DEMYSTIFYING FEMINISM
SMASHING THE PATRIARCHY

DR. SONIA TEOTIA

(MBBS, MD, DNB)

Dedicated to My mother, Mrs. Narinder,

my first teacher and nurturer

Contents

"Women's rights are not a privilege, but a fundamental aspect of human's rights."

- Savitribai Phule (India's first female teacher and noted Indian feminist activist)

Acknowledgements

Dear God, for lighting my path and helping me see and fulfill my dreams.

My mother, to whom this book is dedicated. She set wonderful examples for me, nurtured me, provided me with every comfort of life, and made me the compassionate, independent, wise, sensitive yet strong woman I am today.

My father, who gave me the weapon of education, taught me meticulousness and passed on to me the rational ability to tackle every situation like men can outside the house. I am proud that I file my taxes, know about car servicing and bank work, am not dependent on men to get my work done, and am courageous enough to face challenges even if I am scared.

In a patriarchal society like ours, having progressive feminist parents has been a wonderful blessing.

My husband, who encourages me to fulfill all my goals and dreams, shares my notions of gender equality, is my biggest cheerleader, teaches me new stuff without patronizing, and is the loyal and loving partner I always wanted.

My brother, from whom I learned that there is no substitute for hard work and consistency, and who introduced me to the beautiful world of cinema and its glory.

ACKNOWLEDGEMENTS

My father-in-law, who with his diligent attitude and chilled-out aura makes life seem so simple, progressively shuns societal gender roles and always has interesting anecdotes to share.

My mother-in-law, a very strong, independent, and compassionate woman, a skilled multitasker with the nicest things to say and so much warmth and comfort to offer.

My sister-in-law, an admirable all-rounder, my sweetest friend and confidante.

A bunch of loyal and feminist friends who have been my reliable support system on this journey of life.

All the amazing women and feminist icons outside of family whom I admire.

Peers, students, and patients belonging to all genders whom I have come across, known, observed, psychoanalyzed, and helped.

Preface

"No country can ever truly flourish if it stifles the potential of its women and deprives itself of the contributions of half its citizens."

- Michelle Obama (American attorney & author, former First Lady of the United States)

Feminism is something that everyone has an opinion about, irrespective of intellect and knowledge. As an extroverted and opinionated millennial, I have seen the burden of patriarchal conditioning all around me, first in my peer groups and now in my medical students.

Of course, this isn't absolute, but for the men and women who have consumed this conditioning consciously and subconsciously over their formative years, the battles in later life have turned out to be extra tough.

The topic of feminism triggers those men who feel that all feminists do is male-bashing and playing the woman card, and so they spew hate against this movement. This myth needs to be busted, and everyone needs to know that feminism is simply gender equality, and the reason behind it remaining mostly women-centric in conversations is that women as a gender have a lot of catching up to do with men because of the age-old misogyny that kept dragging them backward.

Feminism is beneficial for men to adopt as a mindset because patriarchy has been unfair towards their existence, growth, evolution, and freedom too, much more than they have been able to realize.

It is worthwhile to mention here that "Achieve gender equality and empower all women and girls" is Sustainable Development Goal #5 of the United Nations.

And what about the LGBTQIA+ community? They have remained downtrodden for so long, though thankfully some recent developments have been in their favor. Intersectional feminism explores the rights of trans women against the background of gender equality.

So dear reader, thanks for picking up my book. I sincerely hope that you either feel understood or evolve to some extent by the end and go on to lead a better life while contributing to a fair society in whatever way may be feasible for you.

1

FEMINISM: THE ACTUAL MEANING

"Life is not a competition between men and women. It is a collaboration."

-David Alejandro Fearnhead (Journalist & author)

Let me cut straight to the chase: feminism is NOT the concept of women being superior to men. It is NOT the concept that advocates for giving women priority over men.

Simply stated, feminism means that women and men are equal in a cerebral sense, and women deserve the same opportunities as men. So basically, it is intertwined with egalitarianism.

An individual's personality and intellectual abilities are a reflection of their nutrition, education, experiences, and social exposure. A man and woman with similar upbringings and privileges may have similar skill sets, so both should be entitled to equal opportunities.

However, there may be situations where the woman is less intellectually sharp than the man. So obviously giving her the job would not be fair. But that shouldn't amount to the strengthening of the stereotype that "women aren't as smart as men".

A comparison would be fair only if the woman in question has also had similar education, experiences, circumstances, and social exposure as the man.

If you examine the childhoods and the history of women who do not exhibit appreciable skill sets and come across as dumb or underconfident, you see how most of them were not empowered by their families and given the freedom to gain worldly experiences.

Lack of their own decision-making and more of following the instructions of others led to wounded self-confidence. Can we, instead of labeling such women as incompetent, address these reasons and give them opportunities to build skill sets?

If not give opportunities, then at least motivate and not shun them? At least not take a jab at their incompetency in many situations?

I discuss the various needs for feminism i.e., gender equality, in this book. How this need arises because of centuries of patriarchal laws and customs that burdened women and men both in starkly different ways.

What were these written and unwritten rules? How diverse were their effects, and how did women get left behind men? Most importantly, how is feminism integral to the formation of a progressive society?

2

THE WAVES OF FEMINISM IN THE WEST

The first wave of feminism (1848-1920) had at its forefront the women's suffrage movement aimed at gaining voting rights for American women. The movement began in July 1848, with a convention organized by Elizabeth Cady Stanton and Lucretia Mott at Seneca Falls, New York.

Attendees signed the Declaration of Sentiments, which affirmed women's equality with men, and passed a dozen resolutions calling for the right to vote, women's education, the right to property, and organizational leadership.

In Britain, the National Society for Women's Suffrage was founded in 1867. Comparable movements spread across the continent over the next three decades.

Even as the wave continued, women of color were often excluded by first-wave feminists and had to continue dealing not just with sexism, but also racism and classism.

The second wave of feminism (1963-1980s) commenced with the publication of The Feminine Mystique in 1963 by Betty Friedan, who discussed how women were being unsatisfactorily confined to the roles of wives and mothers.

Her book sold 3 million copies in three years.

Inspired by the civil rights movement and protests against the Vietnam War, second-wave feminists protested against traditional gender roles in society and sexist discrimination, fighting for women to possess their own bank accounts without the approval of their husbands, and denounced domestic violence and sexual harassment, but are again known to have favored White women.

Some Black women went ahead and formed their own feminist organizations like the National Black Feminist Organization (NBFO).

Legislative milestones in terms of reproductive rights, the right to equal pay, and equal education were attained.

The "third wave" of feminism was announced in 1992 by Rebecca Walker, the daughter of second-wave leader Alice Walker, while watching Anita Hill, an African-American law professor, testify before the Senate Judiciary Committee about her accusations of sexual harassment against Supreme Court nominee Clarence Thomas.

1992, referred to as the "Year of the Woman," witnessed a remarkable number of women elected to Congress. This wave was also more inclusive when it came to race and gender.

Scholar and theorist Kimberlé Crenshaw wrote extensively on the concept of "intersectionality," or how types of oppression (based on race, class, gender, etc.) can overlap and intersect.

Third-wave feminists also made use of the work of gender theorist Judith Butler, and also advocated for trans rights.

The fourth wave of feminism is said to have begun with the advent of the #MeToo movement that took off in 2017 following Alyssa Milano's allegations of sexual misconduct against influential film producer Harvey Weinstein. (Tarana Burke had previously used the phrase "Me Too" for the first time in 2006.)

The internet and social media played a crucial role in popularizing this movement globally, and India saw its own #MeToo movement in late 2018.

3

INDIAN WOMEN'S RIGHTS OVER THE PAST FEW CENTURIES

"Women are regarded as upholding the traditions by conforming to them; men, on the other hand, uphold traditions by enforcing them—not upon themselves but upon women."

— Uma Chakravarti (Author of Gendering Caste: Through a Feminist Lens, Indian Historian & Filmmaker)

Back in the 18th century, Indian women had very scarce agency. Men ruled the society, and very few men advocated for the education of girl children.

There was the vicious evil of the caste system and child marriage that plagued Indian society. Underage girls aged 13-14 years were married off to men triple their age with dowries. They were not educated or financially independent and didn't have family support, as child marriage was a largely unopposed custom.

Once married, these girls were relegated to the status of mere birth machines fit for only domestic chores. They did not have access to good-quality obstetric care either. The shame and taboo around consulting male doctors for obstetric care led to pregnant women dealing with extremes of unhygienic and inhumane conditions during and after their pregnancies.

Young girls who became widows were socially dictated to wear white, shave their heads, remain ostracized, and were denied the right to remarry.

Sati pratha was the traditional Hindu practice of a widow immolating herself on her husband's funeral pyre. It was banned throughout British India by Lord William Bentinck in 1829, and Raja Ram Mohan Roy's persistent efforts had a huge role to play in this. Later, the Sati Prevention Act was enacted by the Government of Rajasthan in 1987 and became an act of the Parliament of India in 1988.

It was in the 19th century that the education scene for Indian women started changing. Among the trailblazers was Peary Charan Sarkar, a former student of Hindu College, Calcutta and a member of 'Young Bengal,' who set up the first free school for girls in India in 1847 in Barasat, a suburb of Calcutta.

Savitribai Phule, who had also been a child bride herself but received an education because of her progressive husband, Jyotirao, went on to become the first female Indian teacher to open a school for girls in Pune, Maharashtra, in 1848. She also contributed significantly to the upliftment of widows and women of oppressed classes.

The Hindu Widow Remarriage Act in 1856 legalized the remarriage of Hindu widows in all the regions under the jurisdiction of the East India Company, aided by the efforts of social reformer Ishwar Chandra Vidyasagar.

Globally, Elizabeth Blackwell became an inspiration for women all over the world in 1865 by becoming the first US woman doctor. This opened the gates of opportunity for more women, and Anandibai Joshi and Kadambini Ganguly became the first two Indian women doctors around 1886.

The former passed away before she could practice, while the latter became a practicing doctor. While both of them were fortunate enough to have husbands who encouraged their education, there were other women pioneers of medical education, like Rukhmabai Raut, who legally challenged her incompatible child marriage and also became one of the major forces behind the Age of Consent Act in 1891, which raised the age of statutory rape for "consenting" Indian brides from 10 years to 12 years.

The women who did break free in that day and age and carved an identity for themselves were able to do so because of progressive fathers, husbands, or their own streak of rebellion and perseverance.

The Child Marriage Restraint Act (Sharda Act) was a legislative act passed in September 1929, which fixed the marriageable age for girls at 14 years and 18 years for boys.

Women's suffrage, i.e., the right of women to vote in elections, was attained after an arduous battle spanning decades. While New Zealand became the first self-governing country in 1893 to grant women the right to vote in Parliamentary elections, limited voting rights in provincial elections for women who met certain property and educational qualifications were introduced in British India in 1919 by the Montagu Chelmsford reforms.

Universal suffrage was, however, granted post-independence at the time of the adoption of the Indian Constitution on January 26, 1950.

As far as property inheritance rights of women are concerned, it was the Hindu Succession (Amendment) Act of 2005 that made significant changes to the 1956 Act and accorded to married women the right to inherit their father's property, which was previously enjoyed only by the male members of the family.

The Prohibition of Child Marriage Act of 2006 fixed the marriageable age for girls at 18 years and for boys at 21 years.

The Indian states of Bihar and Kerala have implemented menstrual leave policies, with Bihar introducing its policy in 1992, allowing women two days of paid menstrual leave each month.

A one-day menstrual leave policy for women workers in both the state government and the private sector was introduced in the Indian state of Odisha in August 2024, and a policy is under consideration in the state of Karnataka. No other state in India offers this leave.

Many private companies and start-ups like Gozoop, Culture Machine, Zomato, Swiggy, and Byju's have also introduced FOP (first day of period) leave.

However, the implementation of these policies comes with its own complications, which I shall discuss in the next chapter.

The Maternity Benefit Act of 1961 has the provision of a paid 26-week maternity leave, extending from 8 weeks before the delivery date to 18 weeks after it.

The sad part, though, is that many private establishments do not incorporate it in their leave policies, though it is enjoyed by most women government employees.

While the 2021 amendment to the Medical Termination of Pregnancy Act stood out as a significant advancement by increasing the gestational limit for legal abortion from 20 to 24 weeks, it did not establish a comprehensive framework for abortion on demand.

Due to the inconsistent interpretation and implementation of abortion laws by various courts, there is a significant obstacle to the equitable access of safe abortion services.

Marital rape has still not been criminalized in India. It is a punishable offense under law in Poland, the UK, the US, Canada, Australia, Sweden, Norway, Denmark, New Zealand, France, Germany, Ireland, Israel, Belgium, Luxembourg, the Netherlands, South Africa, Nepal, and many more countries.

Despite the Dowry Prohibition Act of 1961, dowry deaths in India, where women were tortured and murdered due to unmet dowry demands, continued. Section 498A of the Indian Penal Code (IPC) was introduced in 1983 to safeguard women against violence and dowry in their matrimonial home.

Still, according to the National Crime Records Bureau, 35,493 brides were killed in India between 2017 and 2022—an average of 20 women a day—over dowry demands, sometimes even years after the wedding.

In 2022 alone, more than 6,450 brides were murdered over dowry - that's an average of 18 women every day.

With the introduction of the Bharatiya Nyaya Sanhita (BNS), the provisions of Indian Penal Code Section 498A were split into sections 85 and 86.

Section 85 defines the act of "husband or relative of husband of a woman subjecting her to cruelty," while section 86 outlines the specific acts of cruelty.

The punishment includes up to three years of imprisonment and a fine.

Despite such an available legal option, domestic violence is a recurring and rampant occurrence in many

Indian households.

The anti-domestic violence and anti-dowry laws also need revision, given the data of the past few years, which shows that men are now also at the receiving end of domestic violence.

Alimony is governed by various personal laws, including the Hindu Marriage Act of 1955, the Muslim Personal Law (Shariat) Application Act of 1937, and the Special Marriage Act of 1954.

The current circumstances in the country point towards lacunae in some of the laws, due to many cases of their misutilization against men. I discuss this in greater detail in a later chapter.

This current status of women's basic and legal rights is backed by centuries of struggle. While men mostly enjoyed all sorts of freedom, a significant proportion of women did not have access to education because of patriarchy, even when it became an available option in India.

Furthermore, their quality of life was still dictated by men in their families and social customs and rules. None of this is absolute, but the sad reality is that a lot of bias and discrimination prevails in many households even today.

Knowledge of one's rights comes with education and social exposure, and the power to exercise them is influenced by family support.

So even today, not all women can access legal aid, even if it is available.

Despite so many laws that seemingly guard women, we continue to have a plethora of crimes like dowry deaths, domestic violence, and rape, not followed by consequences in all cases. Women continue to struggle for basic rights at junctures where men have it easy.

4

WOMEN: THE IRONICALLY "WEAKER" GENDER

"You don't know the background story of resilience, struggles, and strength of beautiful and outgoing women. All you see is what is showcased."

- Germany Kent (American journalist, author, actress, producer, and philanthropist)

Owing to their anatomy and physiology, women are menstruators and the child-bearing gender. From menarche to menopause, women with normal physiology get their periods each month.

Along with the bleeding, they endure a variable degree of associated symptoms, including lower abdominal cramps, backache, mood swings, and emotional lability, and women learn to adapt to them and endure these symptoms for an average of 4-5 days each month for approximately 400-500 months during their life.

Then there is the forever unending debate surrounding menstrual leave at workplaces. Women who experience these symptoms deserve rest owing to the physical and emotional challenges.

Imagine having lower abdominal cramps, backache, and heavy bleeding while you sit at your desk, trying to concentrate on your work after popping a painkiller. Or tending to patients and doing surgeries if you are a doctor. Doesn't that sound unfair?

The menstrual leave policies in a few states, mentioned before, are a commendable development and a wonderful comfort for menstruating women. The flip side is that such policies also end up creating barriers to equal opportunities for women. They may be denied certain jobs/projects because of the assumption that since they will be on leave for a day or two each month, their efficiency will also decline.

Also, an important point to be noted here is that not all women may feel equally incapacitated. The women who do not have intense cramps may not avail themselves of their menstrual leave. Nevertheless, there remains a high chance of disparaging chatter from colleagues.

Much more than the struggle of periods are the multitude of mental, emotional, hormonal, and physical changes of pregnancy and the challenges of labor pain, delivery, and postpartum life.

These may be undertaken by enthusiastic women raring to conceive or by women who have no agency in households and have to go through pregnancy not of their own volition but due to family and societal pressure.

Some girls and women conceive as a result of rape. Can we ever imagine their trauma, surrounded by the layered stigma specific to their situation?

The women who decide to stay child-free are judged harshly for the same (sadly, by fellow-women). They are looked down upon and called selfish often by women who are mothers.

There are also plenty of women who are diagnosed with fertility issues who go for assisted reproductive techniques like in vitro fertilization (IVF).

Whether they conceive naturally or not, the pregnancy is endured only by the body of the female.

After giving birth to daughters, many women are coerced to get pregnant again and "try for a boy-child.". Reason? The female gender in many households is considered weaker; daughters are not considered true heirs because they "move away" after marriage, and they are financially tougher to raise because "the dowry system" still prevails under the garb of a custom.

Patriarchy, you see.

In regions with more orthodox ideologies, the hideous, inhuman gore practice of female foeticide continues to prevail.

The cruel murder of a helpless female fetus, wonderfully growing inside the womb of a woman battling with abuse and persecution, who actually wants to deliver the baby girl, incites the decline of her mental health.

The contrasting preference for a boy-child in these households stems from the social tradition of adult sons staying with their parents, carrying forward their family name by having children (again, sons), and offering an additional monetary advantage because their wives would bring along dowry.

Dowry deaths continue in the country despite anti-dowry laws, offering immense challenges for women in households trapped in patriarchal ideologies.

The Maternity Benefit Act of 1961 does provide the right to paid maternity leave, as mentioned before, but remains reserved for women government employees, with many corporate and private establishments excluding it from their leave policies.

Since a married woman might get pregnant at some point, a question regarding the same is mostly posed in her work interviews. Male candidates are hardly questioned about the same, unless they apply for paternity leave.

The Central Civil Services Leave Rule 551 (A), 1972, ensures that eligible male government employees can take 15 days of leave within six months following their child's birth or adoption. The private sector may, however, implement paternity leave at its discretion.

In many households, raising children has also been assumed to be the mother's responsibility. Ali Wong, an actress and mother, voiced the common experience of many women when she said –"It takes very little to be considered a "good dad" and also very little to be considered a "shitty mom.""

Many stay-at-home wives are not given their due respect and credit. Many working women are expected to do a greater amount of housework than their spouses.

To keep themselves safe in a world where they aren't safe almost anywhere, women curtail their own freedom. Not staying out till late for the purpose of work or enjoyment, backing out of opportunities where lecherous men creep them out—there are several such prices that women pay to earn safety for themselves.

All this while, a majority of men enjoy all sorts of freedom without the threat of being molested. Not ruling out the sexual exploitation of men or taking away from the heinous nature of those crimes as well; of course they are just as tragic. But how "commonplace" are these incidents? How often do they make it to the headlines? Are the parents of boys as terrified as the parents of girls?

There are working women who are unable to do evening shifts because that would endanger their safety. The abominable Kolkata case is a recent testament to this.

While overtime would have meant more money and a better quality of life, women have to refrain from it because of their gender. Meanwhile, men easily go ahead with evening and night shifts.

Sexual harassment at the workplace remains a concern and potential threat, significantly more for women than men. I would like to give an example that highlights the huge difference between the fear of being groped and molested in men and women.

A woman waiting for a lift to traverse through many floors will sometimes not enter one full of men, fearing harassment. But would a man do the same if the lift is full of women? How many men would fear violation at the hands of these women?

I do not have a count of the total number of times when, while speaking to me, men ranging from uneducated sweepers to educated clerks to professionals have made me uncomfortable and very angry with their mere gaze. It is in moments like these that my language and tone turn from polite to stern, and I feel the urge to beat them black-and-blue. I make sure I call them out then and there.

In spite of multiple hindrances, women adapt and continue on their journeys as working women, married or not, as mothers, or as stay-at-home wives.

Thankfully, some of these scenarios are changing with the advent of gender equality, conversations around it, women becoming financially and intellectually stronger, recognizing unfair practices, and taking a stand against them.

Education, sisterhood, and strong women predecessors are all encouraging women to claim their seats at the table. After exhibiting so much perseverance, how are women "the weaker gender," the label imposed on them by tradition?

5

STATISTICS I WISH DIDN'T EXIST

"*Men are afraid that women will laugh at them. Women are afraid that men will kill them.*"

-Margaret Atwood (Canadian novelist, poet, and literary critic)

As per the annual National Crime Records Bureau (NCRB) report, between 2017 and 2022, a total of 1.89 lakh rape cases were reported in India, involving 1.91 lakh victims.

In at least 1.79 lakh cases, the rapist was a known person.

Further, the highest number of rape victims in India were between the ages of 18 and 30 years. Of the 1.89 lakh cases, 1.13 lakh were from this age group. Out of the 86 rapes recorded every day, 52 were from the age group between 18 and 30 years.

Further calculation said that every hour, India recorded almost four rape cases, and in more than three of these, the rapist was known to the victim.

There have been cases where the rapist was the school bus driver or teacher or a man with unreciprocated feelings for the victim.

The most horrifying aspect is that there have been many cases where the rapist was a family member of the victim.

In many cases, the rapist also killed the victim brutally.

Turning down a man's proposal, choosing to break up in a relationship—exercising simple choices like these has led to dreadful consequences like acid attacks, rape, and murder for so many women.

Such kinds of statistics reinforce the fact that girls and women aren't safe anywhere.

Women remain vulnerable to rape throughout their lives. Sexual assault is very tough to escape from, because women are physically not as powerful as men.

Rape victims have been baby girls, teenagers, young women, elderly women, women in sarees, women in miniskirts, and women in burqas.

The filthy rapists have spared no one, and so the debate centered around victim-blaming, along the lines of, "What was she wearing? " "Skimpy clothing means she was asking for it" is absolute nonsense and an attempt to divert attention from the real reasons behind rape:

lack of education on consent, young boys and men being introduced to violence against women in their own homes and on unregulated content on the internet, pornography, insecurities of men manifesting as physical aggression and dominance, unequal power equations between the criminals and victims, and lack of a legal framework that guarantees dire consequences, irrespective of how rich and influential the rapist is.

6

PATRIARCHY: ROOTS, INHERITANCE, AND CONDITIONING

"If you educate a man, you educate an individual; however, if you educate a woman, you educate a whole family."

-Pandit Jawaharlal Nehru (India's first Prime Minister)

The Merriam-Webster dictionary defines patriarchy as "social organization marked by the supremacy of the father in the clan or family, the legal dependence of wives and children, and the reckoning of descent and inheritance in the male line."

Simply speaking, it is the mindset that women are inferior and hence cannot enjoy equal rights as men. They cannot have assertive opinions and views and freedom, and much of what they can do will be dictated by the men in the family.

There is male domination and a very obvious gender gap when it comes to power.

In patriarchal households, women are not allowed to date their prospective life partners long enough to make a wise decision regarding marriage; instead, they are married off hastily, saying that there is plenty of time to understand the husband after marriage.

What happens to many such marriages? They crumble under the weight of incompatibility, surprises, and adjustment borne out of helplessness.

Worse still, in some regions, the barbaric practice of "honor killing" involves the killing of daughters who are believed to have brought "dishonor" to the family by getting romantically involved with or married to men whom the family disapproves of.

The social evil of dowry is also a byproduct of patriarchy. While there are people who oppose this custom with their progressive views, it does continue in both occult and ostentatious ways in many other households. I know many women whose parents gave dowry, and seeing it so commonplace leaves me horrified. Why would you pay someone to marry your daughter? In a dowry situation, both families have to be staunch believers of patriarchy.

My family and I always had strong anti-dowry opinions and so did my husband and in-laws, and we shall make sure that no one in our family succumbs to this social evil, ever.

In many regressive households, women may not enjoy the freedom of wearing clothes of their choice, or consent in a physical relationship, or have the right to an abortion, or have the freedom to pursue their academic and professional ambitions, with men in the family controlling these aspects.

A well-known YouTuber, Lilly Singh, settled in the UK, having her roots in Punjab, India, an outspoken feminist in today's times, was describing in her TED Talk how the news of her birth brought sadness to her parents' family back in India because she was a "girl," born after her sister.

When a woman stands on a celebrated platform like TED and describes this slice of gender inequality, millions of women worldwide relate to it. This brings them together, stronger as a community, to address and fight the gender stereotypes they have grown up with, demanding their worth by virtue of their talents, qualifications, and skills. And NOT denied to them because of their gender.

After being assigned a gender at birth, what follows is upbringing dictated by protocols reserved for each gender.

A rampant societal bias has existed when it comes to education, as discussed before. The negligent attitude towards the education of the girl child is not confined to rural settings. It exists in a cleverly veiled fashion in some urban households too. Fortunately not in all.

Sometimes, even if the parents are progressive and encourage higher education of their daughters, there is a certain nosy relative who condemns it as unimportant under the pretext of what to them is the ultimate destiny of women: raising children.

A demarcation between the "normal" behaviors of girls and boys in early childhood, determined by their parents, sets the tone of the gender stereotypes they carry with them into their teenage and adult years.

These learned behaviors and concepts, which have formed deep impressions on the psyche of the children, are referred to as conditioning.

The exclusive motivation of boys to play outdoor sports while restricting girls to playing with dolls and indoor board games is one such stereotype. Assuming meltdowns and tears in unfavorable situations are a default "normal" reaction of girls while chiding boys for expressing their feelings or shedding tears and introducing them to warped notions of emotional expression is a close second. More on this later.

At an age when a child can assist in safe, basic household chores, training only the girl child in helping with setting the dining table, fetching anyone a glass of water, making the bed, doing one's own laundry, and cleaning up after oneself is setting the tone for the friendships and relationships the girl will have in the future.

Who trains these girls to do this? Usually the mothers or elderly females of the household. These women heard similar things in their own childhood, followed them all their lives, and now are passing them as concepts to the amateur brains of the girls. Many of these women despite being highly educated, are unable to recognize the flaws in their conditioning. The young daughters see the silent endurance of their mothers towards unfair practices and absorb the absurd glorification of their sacrifices.

All this while the other observer –"the boy child" in these households—is slowly, at a subconscious level, developing a sense of entitlement where he feels that all the household work, which is essential for everybody's survival, is somehow the exclusive duty of the women in the household.

Hence, patriarchy, existing since times immemorial, is learnt at home, absorbed religiously, and practiced liberally throughout life (introjection), unless better sense prevails.

Unless as adults, humans come to possess the intelligence to look back and realize the wrong practices that happened back home, they may not change.

If they do, (which so many people around me have), then they contribute to an evolved and progressive society.

In today's times, social media has brought the world so much closer. We know the campaigns, the ideas, the protests, and the awakenings happening on a global level with explicit detail at the mere clicking of links and conduct of Google searches.

It has become easier to learn new things, introspect, change, and move with the times, unless one is a really stubborn bigot, of course.

The progressive ones easily spot and bond with people going through similar struggles, unite for societal causes, and practice sisterhood and women empowerment.

7
WOMEN'S SENSE OF SELF -WORTH

"A man told me that for a woman, I was very opinionated. I said, 'For a man, you're kind of ignorant.'"

- Anne Hathaway (American actress, Academy Award winner)

As an Indian who was very much absorbed into social media in my early 20s, I did not come across the word feminism till I turned 27.

A lot of my peers were having disagreements in relationships, at home, and at work owing to a visibly unfair gender bias, ridiculous gender roles, and assumed responsibilities dictated solely by their gender. So conversations had started happening.

Many women had started saying that some things they were being told were wrong.

Ask yourself at this point, did you face anything similar? Did you, during phases of silent people-pleasing and conforming to the roles dictated to you, have an epiphany that you were being abused by a rule that was a construct of the society?

As I took on the role of a teacher during my medical residency, I saw that in many families, children had grown up around adults weighed down by their own patriarchal conditioning, who passed it on to them.

The conditioning at home and school largely contributed to a myopic mindset of stereotypes labelling girls/women as comparatively less intellectual and mentally weaker than boys/men.

It could get disastrously orthodox, depending on home to home. In many homes, it included girls being told not to speak up in their homes before their brothers and fathers when they had dysmenorrhea (spasmodic lower abdominal pain because of uterine cramps).

This instilled a sense of embarrassment in girls, making them feel awkward about an involuntary physiological process, which added a mental distress component to the already prevalent physical distress of periods.

I found their sense of embarrassment surprising because this had never happened in my home, maybe because I come from a medical background.

Periods are a necessity for a functioning reproductive system. This same system is a manufacturer of babies, which are also a societal expectation in many homes after a girl gets married.

But in so many households, illiterate and literate alike, there are still nonsensical beliefs that a woman on her period is "impure"—so she should not sit in the temple, she should not enter the kitchen, and in rural areas this extends to the ridiculous custom of her sleeping away from the comfort of her own bed as long as her periods last.

The same woman is often pampered when she is pregnant by the same women who had imposed the regressive aforementioned customs on her.

The growing fetus is attached now to a thickened endometrial lining of the uterus, and the whole world can see her carrying the fetus in the last trimester, yet when this lining was sloughing off in her non-gravid days, she was being made to feel "impure."

The correct mindset would be to be nice to menstruating women, as nice as you would be to the expecting ones. Be considerate about their mood swings, their pain, and their comfort, and for God's sake—let women TALK ABOUT IT!!!

The way a girl is treated by her father and brother and how her father treats her mother contribute substantially to the type of behavior that she willingly "accepts" from her male friends/partner/husband. This is a well-established psychological pattern and also extends to girls with absent fathers subconsciously choosing emotionally unavailable partners.

A woman's sense of self-worth is very much a reflection of the emotional quality of her childhood. I see hapless girls among my students, freshly out of their teens, in abusive relationships in their early 20s, and conversations make me discover the childhood trauma and faulty parenting that has culminated in these immature decisions.

Many girls who are not taught the concept of "good touch" and "bad touch" fall prey to molestation in childhood. Their amateur minds cannot even interpret these incidents properly, with often their own family members (even mothers) asking them to brush these conversations under the carpet.

Such mothers are usually those who have grown up trapped in misogynistic households and have most probably been married into similar ones too.

They lack agency; they feel hesitant and underconfident in discussing these matters because somewhere they feel that these situations spell shame for the victims and their families.

While the only person who should feel shame and should be punished is the perpetrator, but it is the victims who walk away with psychological trauma.

In many households in India, girls are raised as a liability because of the social custom of them relocating to their husband's house post-marriage.

Parents and relatives voice this to them throughout their childhood without realizing how their dumping of generational trauma is impacting the self-worth of the girl.

How can society progress if we keep dragging our daughters back, denying them freedom and equality? How will better sense prevail in our future generations if we do not address these social and cultural vices right now?

Shouldn't subsequent generations be wiser, more open-minded, egalitarian, and intellectually stronger with each person, irrespective of gender, believing that they are capable of achieving anything that they want?

How can we expect this to happen if we keep raising our girls in a pool of patriarchy and misogyny?

We need to inculcate confidence and independence in our girls right from childhood. It includes, but shouldn't remain limited to, teaching them basic survival skills and small chores along with their brothers, educating them, and telling them that their ambitions and careers are equally important as their male peers.

The financial independence of women ensures agency in relationships and gives them the choice of leaving abusive and incompatible marriages without having to depend on anyone else.

Parents must teach their daughters how to draw strong boundaries and not indulge in people-pleasing, practice emotional regulation from a young age, and never tell them that their parents' house is not their real home.

Parents of daughters should consider themselves at par with the groom's family while marrying their daughters and rise above the social obligation of "the bride's family must remain subordinate to the groom's family."

Only this can incite a change in the traditional dynamic of married couples that has prevailed in many regressive households over time.

8

"NOT ALL WOMEN"

There are many types of women in the world. One type is stubborn women who have been at the receiving end of unfair conditioning and patriarchy and have their mindsets aligned with the same. They haven't been able to recognize the behavior meted out to them as "wrong," and they actually pass it on to the women in their radius, like their daughters and daughters-in-law and women at their workplaces.

These women can have harrowing views like "women need to dress modestly to avoid the male gaze" or "women shouldn't date, but that's a given for men" and "dating defines the character of women" or "women shouldn't talk back to men" or "men by default should have the upper hand in a marriage" or "married women shouldn't support their parents financially and are duty bound to serve the in-laws, but c'mon, men don't follow these rules!! " Or worse still, "men, by virtue of their hormones, are adulterers".

My personal way to handle such women is to steer absolutely clear of them. Back in the day, I would blindly support them as victims of their conditioning and try to sympathize and show them the lacunae in their views, but time made me realize that many of these women cannot be salvaged; they emit a toxic negative energy intertwined with the envious shaming of evolved independent women.

Negative experiences trying to change such women have made me extremely selective about my aura, and I no longer engage with them if their intellectual wavelength is not in sync with mine.

Of course you may feel differently. You may feel like we need to start with the victims if we want all genders to evolve and weave and wear the fabric of feminism. But as I mentioned, my mantra in this regard stems from a lot of experience with such women—there are high chances that you will drain yourself and get exhausted in the process.

Another type is women who think like me and have been fortunate enough to be in the midst of feminist parents and relatives and have turned out independent and capable of helping others in need.

Similarly, there are women who faced biases but were intellectually sharp and open to challenging them once they were introduced to the concepts of patriarchy and gender equality because of real-life observations, social media, and the fine arts.

These women know their worth and tear down societal barriers. They uplift the women who are trying to rise but are struggling with their means. [These are a separate type, can be spotted fighting for their identity, but might be tolerating biases because of fear and lack of motivating peers, family, or circumstances. I happily take such women under my wing. It is the inflexible and prejudiced ones that I avoid].

These are women who will be happy for other women, who will break the stereotypes of "women being each other's enemy," which has prevailed for decades now thanks to the first type of women.

Another type is women who have taken the whole gender debate to a narcissistic level and have emerged as feminazis. Simply put, these are women who consider themselves superior to men, and in their wrath, they go around trashing men.

They jump on the bandwagon of "women are not taking shit anymore and are speaking up" to fulfill their ulterior motives of fame, revenge, or monetary gains.

Let me illustrate this with some examples. A woman not getting a promotion may come up with a plan to expedite her promotion by engaging in false mudslinging of her colleague.

She could falsely accuse him of workplace harassment, leading to the sacking and shaming of the man, as the woman in such a situation will garner the sympathy of a majority.

The man will face humiliation and embarrassment and will have to deal with disturbed mental health and its repercussions.

A woman can also opt for a similar calculated strategy to settle some other personal vendetta, thereby fulfilling her goal of revenge. The goal for another woman may be fame.

I once had a friend with whom I would bond over shared feminist opinions. We often discussed how men have had it easy and women have had to struggle for basic rights.

Surprisingly, once she said something to the effect of, "What is the big deal if an innocent guy has to deal with the label of a bad guy? This is the least he can do to make up for the actual bad things that other guys have done before him."

Thankfully I had the mental clarity to address the hypocrisy of this train of thought against the fair background of feminism.

As a feminist, I have neither believed that men are superior to women nor have I believed in the opposite. I have simply advocated that women should get the same rights and opportunities and treatment as men.

Both should respect each other and not take undue advantage of the feminist movement. This shall only discredit the movement and fuel the already existing resistance against it by orthodox minds.

•

9

MEN AND PATRIARCHY

"A world full of empowered women isn't one where men are marginalized. It's a world where everyone thrives."

- Purnima Mane (President and CEO of Pathfinder International)

While it is not possible as a woman to ignore the many privileges granted to men solely because of their gender, it is very important to talk about a seldom-discussed matter: how patriarchy impacts men.

The chronicles of patriarchal conditioning can be traced to the times when many baby boys are intentionally not clothed in socially labelled feminine colors like "pink". While this seems harmless, many are encouraged to play outdoors much more than girls and not taught to assist in age-appropriate chores around the house as they grow up.

They may develop the opinion that housework and kitchen work is the responsibility of the females in the house, and once married, may expect their wives to conform accordingly. In this way, financially independent men may not become independent in the real sense.

When boys express their emotions, especially through tears, many of them are often shunned, shamed, or dismissed and told to "toughen up" because "boys and men don't cry."

Such men resort to isolation or aggression in times of conflict, rather than meaningful communication and expression. Stressful situations may also cause them to internalize this stress and let it fester.

Ever wondered about the gender gap in the number of heart attacks and suicide rates, with strikingly more cases among men? This plays a huge factor there.

Children need immense care, and the environment at home must be monitored wisely. Domestic violence towards mothers can have a deleterious effect on the impressionable young son's mind, somewhere instilling in him the notion that this behavior towards women is acceptable and imitable.

Teaching boys the basic etiquette of respecting everyone and not objectifying girls and women is the sole responsibility of the parents. So is teaching them about consent and respecting it.

Patriarchy ends up teaching them that they are superior to women and so must dominate them, and this domination paves the path for the violation of consent, suppression of women and their rights, and hating on more successful women, and makes it difficult for such men to even work under better-qualified women at professional workplaces.

While patriarchy conditions men into believing that their masculinity is defined by the power that they have in their relationships with women, it also equates their worth with the money that they earn, and this is evident during the process of matchmaking, especially in arranged marriage settings.

Not just this; this pressure on men also blends with the societal expectation of sons taking sole financial responsibility for their parents. There are men wanting to become entrepreneurs, but they cannot take financial risks because what if society labels them as worthless sons?

In this regard, patriarchy gives girls an unquestioned leeway, because it no longer considers them as an integral part of their parental family anymore once they are married.

Patriarchy recommends a power play in marriages; for example, some parents may disapprove of a girl who is more qualified than their son when it comes to marriage.

They may prefer a girl who is less qualified, wants to remain a homemaker, in the hope of her being demure and submissive as she will be financially dependent on their son.

When such marriages crumble among Hindus, then one of the deciding factors of alimony according to the

Hindu Marriage Act of 1955 is the qualification and employment of both the individuals. This entitles the women to alimony.

If both the individuals are earning well and are independent, this would reduce the burden of alimony on the man. How many people, however, consider THIS while engaging in the alimony debate?

In order to lead better lives emotionally and socially, men too need to escape from the clutches of patriarchy. They must develop insight, break generational patriarchal patterns, and raise their girls and boys without gender biases.

10

THE FREQUENTLY OVERLOOKED PROBLEMS OF MEN

"You cannot insult a man more atrociously than by refusing to believe he is suffering."

-Cesare Pavese (Italian novelist, poet, literary critic, and essayist)

When we discuss the legal rights of men and women, it is a multifaceted framework. While we have a multitude of women who face domestic violence, and dowry demands and approach our courts for justice, sadly we also have several others who make false allegations of violence or dowry against their husbands and many others who also take undue advantage of alimony laws and exploit their husbands.

Since women have been at the receiving end of violence since times immemorial, when there is any fresh allegation against a husband, the consensus labels him the villain. The wife is hardly subjected to scrutiny.

The reality of the exploitation of women overshadows the incidents where men are falsely implicated; the scales tip in favor of the women, and these men and their plight often goes unheard.

Violence against men ranges from verbal, physical, emotional, and psychological to sexual. They encounter multiple deterrents while speaking up about it, starting from the social stigma and mockery associated with being subservient in a male-dominated society; a consequence of patriarchy.

Then, of course, they also have their reservations with the expression of their feelings and trauma, owing to their conditioning regarding maintaining a tough exterior.

Also, since domestic violence against men isn't recognized as an offense by Indian law yet, men think there is no benefit in being vocal about violence.

There are also false accusations of dowry demands, again a matter in which only women are protected under sections 85 and 86 of the Bharatiya Nyaya Sanhita (BNS) (formerly 498A of the IPC).

Five laws govern alimony in India: the Hindu Marriage Act of 1955, the Muslim Personal Law Application Act of 1937, the Indian Divorce Act of 1869, the Parsi Marriage and Divorce Act of 1936, and the Special Marriage Act of

1954.

Section 24 and section 25 of The Hindu Marriage Act of 1955 deal with temporary and permanent alimony, respectively. Alimony among Hindus is gender neutral, with the primary determinants being the seeking spouse's financial need and the paying spouse's financial capacity.

Basic needs of the wife and children in the future, qualification and employment of both individuals, the standard of living of the wife while living with her in-laws, and whether she had left her job to take care of the family are among the other determinants.

While these laws provide a necessary relief for needy women post-divorce, a few greedy women with ulterior motives find their way around these laws, and the involved men undergo mental and financial harassment.

A prominent case in India was of Atul Subhash, a software engineer based in Bangalore, who committed suicide in December 2024. Prior to it, he recorded an 81-minute video and wrote a 24-page suicide note, detailing his emotional and financial harassment at the hands of his wife and in-laws, due to false allegations of cruelty and harassment for dowry, demands of unreasonable alimony, unreasonable financial demands to withdraw the false cases against him, and denial to meet his four-year-old son. His suicide was followed by a natural outcry on social media , and I, of course strongly condemn the circumstances that pushed him towards suicide. Information on many similar cases is just a google click away.

The National Crime Records Bureau (NCRB) data revealed a total of 170,924 suicides in India during 2022. Among these, 122,724 victims were males, 48,172 were females, and 28 were transgenders.

67% of the suicide victims were married while 24.6% were unmarried.

If observed closely, the burden of patriarchy is responsible for sexism and the lower educational status of women, who then remain financially weaker than men in marriages.

As stated before, in the event of separation, these women become eligible for alimony as the financially weaker spouse, and depending on their demeanor, they may try to exploit the situation.

However, if women receive education at par with men, and the two partners are financially strong, courts may rule out the need for alimony.

Gender equality advocates for gender-neutral laws against harassment and domestic violence in India because everyone has the right to justice, irrespective of gender.

Also, introducing pre-nuptial agreements before marriage can be a wise approach to safeguarding the men's assets and rights in the event of separation.

11

"NOT ALL MEN"... IN THE WAKE OF #MeToo

—————⟡—————

"I know enough women who are totally patriarchal, who are totally anti-women, who do nasty things to other women, and I have known men who have worked for women's rights their whole life. Feminism is not biological. Feminism is an ideology."

-Kamla Bhasin (Indian developmental feminist activist, poet, author and social scientist)

The #MeToo movement gained prominence in 2017 after actress Alyssa Milano encouraged women to use the hashtag #MeToo on Twitter in response to news reports of sexual abuse by Harvey Weinstein.

In India, it began in late 2018 and gained prominence after Bollywood actor Tanushree Dutta accused actor Nana Patekar of sexual misconduct. This was followed by several allegations against men in the public eye—filmmakers, actors, YouTubers, and singers.

Many of them also had to face consequences (thankfully), and their roles in their respective projects were terminated, setting scary examples for other lecherous men.

Some of the accused also received support and continued to get work despite the allegations, much to everyone's horror.

I often wonder about those men who were falsely accused and vilified and underwent trauma because of the same. Their reputation was tarnished at a time when the movement was in full swing, and they tried their best to recover during and after legal battles.

In the aftermath of the horrifying Kolkata female doctor rape case in August 2024, the internet was flooded with angry, scared women, screaming about the incident and talking about their own fearful experiences in their workplaces, homes, while commuting, or in relationships.

As rape cases of more girls and women started coming to light, there was also an uprise in the incidents of violence and assault on doctors.

As hospitals and medical colleges in India took to protests on and off-premises, demanding safety for women and doctors, a lot of the country's population plunged into horror and fear.

Women at that time became much more triggered than usual. I also felt the undercurrent of an unreasonable loathing as I saw any unknown man, even on the streets.

I looked around and saw many parents fearful and distressed, with their children studying in distant colleges.

I saw rape victims going through PTSD as the graphic details trending everywhere refused to become any less explicit.

Influencers used their platforms to educate and mobilize people.

Some of my students, who were now doing residency or had just taken exams for postgraduate med school, looked apprehensively at a medical system oblivious to what it would bring their way.

I tried to guide them regarding the criteria for choosing their colleges by gathering relevant information.

In a digital turn of events, the narrative changed to men vs. women as the hashtag #AllMen started trending on various platforms, notably Twitter.

Most women expressed that to them, every man seemed a potential rapist. They took care to exclude their fathers and/or brothers.

Men on the platforms defended their gender and expressed how it was wrong to extend the bashing to the entire gender, calling for the mudslinging to be reserved only for the perpetrators.

Women had comebacks to this too, saying, "We are all triggered right now, so just offer us patience and listen.

Please don't start defending men when we tell you how we are feeling."

Akin to most women, I had also faced eve-teasing, fear in lifts, and around strange men in some public places. I felt a misplaced anger during celebrations of the ironic Independence Day of 2024 , wondering how independent our women citizens really are; with the frightening details of the Kolkata case running through my mind.

In the midst of angsty women, I also felt a lot of angst.

But all of this—can it ever justify the hate towards "all" men because we don't know which ones are good? No, that would be extremely unfair towards the genuinely good men in my life.

So, yes, I am a feminist, but I am not siding with the narrative of #AllMen. Yes, I'd feel unsafe with every male stranger in a deserted place, but never around the men in my family, and for that reason, my hashtag would always be #NotAllMen.

I do, however, understand that there are also victims of sexual abuse who have had unfortunate, traumatic experiences with men in their own family, and these women will have completely different views on this topic.

I would like to express my relief and gratitude towards all the men of good character that I have encountered in my life, starting from my family. The world will continue to need more of you.

12

FEMINIST INDIAN POETRY, LITERATURE, AND CINEMA

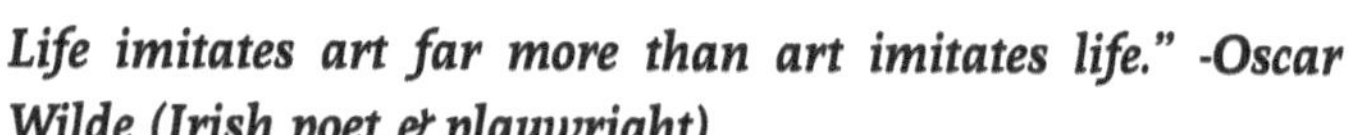

Life imitates art far more than art imitates life." -Oscar Wilde (Irish poet & playwright)

I take immense pride in the evolution of Indian fine arts and performing arts.

India has produced many feminist icons who observed and wrote about gender inequality and their own experiences with patriarchy and became a source of inspiration for future generations.

Growing up, I mostly read James Hadley Chase, Enid Blyton, Jane Austen, Shakespeare, and Sidney Sheldon. It was in my mid 20s that I started reading the works of Indian female authors, which were not so popular among my peer groups.

A pioneer in many ways, Savitribai Phule also wrote poetry about her struggles, which was published as the compilations titled Kavya Phule (1854) and Bavan Kashi Subodh Ratnakar (1892).

Tarabai Shinde's Stri Purush Tulana (1882), apparently the first modern Indian feminist text, compares the differences in the lives of men and women in those times.

Rassundari Devi's autobiography, Amar Jiban (1876), described her struggle for education as a Bengali woman in the 19th century.

Sarojini Naidu wrote extensively about women's empowerment alongside her political journey and role in the independence movement.

Pandita Ramabai in her book High Caste Hindu Woman (1887), exposed the types of gender oppression disguised as tradition and customs.

Urmila Pawar's book The Weave of My Life (1988) offered commendable insights on intersectional feminism.

There was also Cornelia Sorabji, the first woman to read law at Oxford, who wrote Love and Life Behind the Purdah (1901) and Shubala: A Child-Mother (1920).

Sultana's Dream (1905) by Rokeya Shekhawat Hossain imagined a world dominated by women, and makes for a thought-provoking read.

The Progressive Writers Movement, saw the contributions of post-Independence writers like Amrita Pritam [Pinjar (1950) and Raseedi Ticket (1976)], among several others.

The independent publishing house "Kali for Women," set up by Urvashi Butalia and Ritu Menon in 1984, paved the way for Indian feminist literature.

Along with Zubaan Books and Women Unlimited, it published various women writers, such as Manjula Padmanabhan, Bulbul Sharma, and Vandana Shiva.

Anita Desai's In Custody (1984) and Manju Kapur's Difficult Daughters (1998) stand out as hard-hitting literature.

Kamla Bhasin authored gems like Some Questions on Feminism and its Relevance in South Asia (1986), What is Patriarchy (1993), and Understanding Gender (2000).

Uma Chakravarti's Gendering Caste through a Feminist Lens (2003), Kumkum Roy's Women in Early Indian Societies (1999) and The Power of Gender and the Gender of Power (2010), Salma's The Hour Past Midnight (2009), and Ambai's A Night with a Black Spider: Stories (2017) are among my favorites.

Bama's Karukku (1992) and Meena Kandasamy's When I Hit You (2017) are some examples of an intersectional approach in contemporary feminist writing, revealing the unique struggles Dalit women face.

Baby Haldar's A Life Less Ordinary (2006) is also a compelling read.

From a time when content centered around gender equality was either misrepresented or remained within the confines of parallel cinema to now, when commercial cinema also discusses these subjects through an unbiased lens, we have come a long way.

Indian women-centric cinema includes Arth (1982), which showed us the journey of a woman on the path of self-discovery and self-love after discovering her husband's extramarital affair.

Paa (2009) had a single mother raising a child with progeria against all odds.

Ishqiya (2010) and Dedh Ishqiya (2014) had interesting character arcs of strong, conniving women with ulterior motives.

Queen (2014) showed us the transformation of a demure and wilfully submissive woman to an independent, self-loving, liberated woman following abandonment by her fiancée.

Chak De India (2007) explored the interpersonal conflicts and camaraderie between women hockey players as their coach strived to exonerate his negative image.

Kahaani (2012), an amazing thriller, was the journey of a wife in search of her missing husband and showed the extent of the strength of a hurting woman.

Thappad (2019) insisted that violence, irrespective of its frequency, should qualify as a deal-breaker in marriage.

Darlings (2022) also dealt with domestic violence and its potential aftermath.

The Great Indian Kitchen (2021) was a hard-hitting portrayal of a woman stuck in a regressive marriage and her escape.

Lipstick Under My Burkha (2016) was an ensemble movie that showed the trials and tribulations of different women who fought back against societal stereotypes and patriarchy.

Tribhanga (2021) discussed generational trauma as it broached the delicate subject of faulty parenting by mothers (for a change).

Mrs. Undercover (2023) approached the topic of housewives not getting due credit and how every woman can channel their inner strength to fight against evil, if need be.

Panga (2020) showed how mothers face typical internal conflicts and societal backlash when they start out to carve an identity for themselves outside their relationships.

English Vinglish (2012) showed how a mother can be strong and sensitive at the same time and how she can fight back against patriarchy and reclaim her identity.

The recent Sharmaajee Ki Beti (2024) was a refreshing visual treat, exploring the themes of parenting, feminism, and the LGBT community.

OTT platforms also make web series available globally. According to me, the best Indian series that dissected gender equality was "Man's World.". It was released back in 2015, and to date, I recommend it as an educational material on this topic.

13

THE LGBTQIA+ COMMUNITY: RIGHTS AND REPRESENTATION

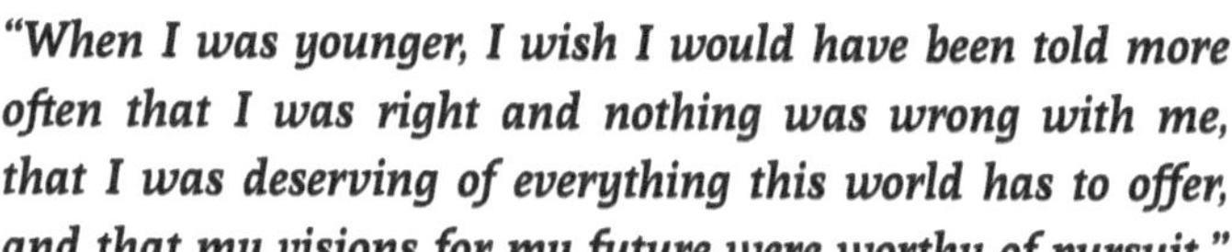

"When I was younger, I wish I would have been told more often that I was right and nothing was wrong with me, that I was deserving of everything this world has to offer, and that my visions for my future were worthy of pursuit."

-Janet Mock (New York Times bestselling author, speaker, director and advocate)

In a society where women and men already have to fight against a deeply engrained patriarchal mindset, body shaming, complexion shaming, and outdated beliefs; a huge chunk of people around me (a Tier-2 city) hardly even know the expansion of the acronym of LGBTQIA+, let alone understand the constant struggles of people belonging to these communities.

For the unfamiliar, this acronym stands for Lesbian, Gay, Bisexual, Transgender, Queer (or questioning), Intersex, and Asexual.

The LGBTQIA+ community has existed since time immemorial, with their mention in some scriptures as well.

Despite some Indian laws in their favor, this community continues to undergo struggles for acceptance and freedom in our society.

From not being accepted by their families to being forced to live without being open about their identity, many people of this community have been expelled from schools or had to leave their families at a young age and turn to unsafe means of earning a livelihood.

Many homosexual individuals have to enter into the arrangement of lavender marriages, because of unacceptance by their families and fear of the social stigma after coming out of the closet.

Sadly, even the educated are ill-informed about LGBTQIA+ terminologies. I have heard all sorts of half-baked opinions from educated peers and seen massive discrimination against them at workplaces.

An honest insight into their lives can be achieved by reading their books.

Manobi Bandopadhyay and Living Smile Vidya have written about their personal stories, highlighting the struggles of the transgender community.

The Truth About Me: A Hijra Life Story (2010) by A. Revathi also qualifies as a compassion-evoking read, and so does We Are Not the Others: Reflections of a Transgender Artivist (2021) by Kalki Subramaniam.

A significant milestone was attained in 2014 when the Supreme Court of India delivered a judgment recognizing the transgender (TG) community as a third gender.

In 2018, the Supreme Court of India decriminalized Section 377 of the IPC. However, since same-sex marriage in India is not legalized, LGBTQIA+ couples are denied many social and legal benefits of marriage, such as inheritance, adoption, insurance, and pension.

Growing up, I mostly saw the LGBTQIA+ community being reduced to objects of ridicule and comic relief in cinema and television with unfair stereotyping, along with the characters mostly being dehumanized and having ill-developed character arcs.

Their representation has undergone a commendable change, with plenty of projects in parallel cinema as well as some commercial movies and many web series also showcasing their struggles and journeys.

I believe that a large proportion of Indians/people receive their preliminary education and priming about the LGBTQIA community via OTT platforms.

After all, not everyone is intellectual enough to google, read, or follow the news, but watching a movie or a series seems easier and less taxing on the mind.

The process of mental engagement with good storylines may produce compassion or evoke empathy and enable the humanization of characters shown as members of the LGBTQIA community.

Such movies include My Brother Nikhil, Dedh Ishqiya, Aligarh, Kapoor & Sons, Ek Ladki Ko Dekha To Aisa Laga, Margarita With A Straw, Shubh Mangal Zyada Saavdhan, Badhaai Do, Chandigarh Kare Aashiqui, Kaathal-The Core, and Bhool Bhulaiyaa 3.

These movies starred progressive Indian artists like Sanjay Suri, Juhi Chawla, Manoj Bajpayee, Kalki Koechlin, Rajkummar Rao, Fawad Khan, Sonam Kapoor, Ayushmann Khurrana, Jitendra Kumar, Bhumi Pednekar, Vaani Kapoor, Jyothika, Mammootty, Vidya Balan, and Kartik Aryan, who brought the well-written characters to life.

A renowned Indian filmmaker, Karan Johar, broached the subject of homosexuality in a movie starring Randeep Hooda, Rani Mukherjee, and Saqib Saleem that was a part of the 2013 anthology Bombay Talkies.

One movie in the anthology of Ajeeb Daastaans, speaking about homosexuality, featured Konkana Sen Sharma and Aditi Rao Hydari in pivotal roles.

The web series Murder in Mahim, starring Vijay Raaz and Ashutosh Rana, based on the novel of the same name by Jerry Pinto, is a recent favorite of mine, followed by a close second, Taali, featuring Sushmita Sen as the transgender activist Shreegauri Sawant.

The recent series Maja Maa starring the ethereal Madhuri Dixit was a great watch too.

It is imperative to understand that the LGBTQIA+ community also deserves all the rights enjoyed by men and women and no one deserves hate and intolerance because of their particular sexual orientation or gender.

Their struggles have been immense, from being mocked and discriminated against to being ostracized and not having basic amenities that you and I take for granted.

Not downplaying their struggles, not bullying them in schools, creating inclusive education and workplace opportunities for them, supporting them in their fights for their rights, and considering them as human as you and me – are some of the efforts we can make to bring about a difference.

14

MEN & WOMEN IN TODAY'S INDIA

"There is an urgent need to tackle the ills of the society against women through active participation of all—men, women, and society and governments. It is imperative to make women empowerment a people's movement."

- Sushma Swaraj (Indian lawyer, politician, and diplomat who served as the former Chief Minister of Delhi and also the Minister of External Affairs of India)

Indian girls and women continue to fight against patriarchy and misogyny even today. Still, they also enjoy many rights and opportunities, thanks to many women and few men predecessors, who relentlessly fought for women's rights.

The current status of women in India is a reflection of many things: the prevailing burden of patriarchy, the perseverance of girls and women despite it, and the changing mindsets of many parents who have raised their children without inculcating gender biases.

India has had two female Presidents (Mrs. Pratibha Patil and Mrs. Droupadi Murmu) and only one female Prime Minister (Mrs. Indira Gandhi) since Independence in 1947, and several other women ministers over the years.

The sworn-in members of the 18th Lok Sabha include 74 women MPs (Members of Parliament), which is the highest share ever recorded.

Seven women, including Nirmala Sitharaman, Annapurna Devi, and Anupriya Singh Patel, are a part of the current Union Council of Ministers.

According to the Ministry of Statistics and Programme Implementation (MoSPI), in the 2011 Census, India's population was 121.1 crore, with 48.5% being females.

The literacy rate at all levels in India steadily increased from 18.32% in 1951 to 72.98% in 2011, and the increase in literacy rates for females and males was from 8.86% and 27.15% to 64.63% and 80.9%, respectively, as per the last population census conducted in 2011.

The Ministry of Statistics and Programme Implementation (MoSPI), Government of India, released the 25th issue of its publication titled "Women and Men in India 2023" last year.

This publication statistically reflects the status of gender disparity in India and takes into account factors like population, education, health, and participation in the economy, among others.

It states that by 2036, the population of India is expected to reach 152.2 crore, with a slightly improved female percentage of 48.8% as compared to 48.5 percent in 2011.

As per data of National Sample Surveys conducted by MoSPI, the gender gap in literacy rate went down from 18.2 in 2007-08 to 14.4 in 2017-18.

The literacy rate of females is more than that of males only in urban Assam, and the gender gap is the lowest in Kerala at 2.2.

Though the literacy rates are not very encouraging for the entire population, it is not the case with youth. As per the 75th Round of National Sample Surveys during 2017-18, the literacy rate in the age group of 15-24 years is more than 90% with a gender gap of less than 5 percentage points.

Gross Enrolment Ratio (GER) is the total enrolment in a particular level of school education, regardless of age, expressed as a percentage of the population of the official age-group that corresponds to the given level of school education in a given school year.

The GER of female children has always been higher than that of male children at the primary level, at least from 2012-13 onwards.

A decreasing trend can be seen in GER as we move to higher levels of education, viz. upper primary, secondary, and higher secondary in the case of both males as well as females.

From 2012-13 to 2021-22, the number of female teachers per 100 males at the primary level increased from 100 to 126. A similar trend was seen at the higher levels too.

However, the representation of females in tertiary education teachers is comparatively lower at 41.6 % as per 2021-22 data.

In the fiscal year 2022-23, the WPR (Worker Population Ratio) for the male population was 54 in rural areas and 55.6 in urban areas, while for the female population, it was significantly lower at 30 in rural and 18.7 in urban areas.

For the population aged 15 years and above, the WPR for males was 78.0 in rural areas and 71.0 in urban areas. In stark contrast, the corresponding figures for females were 40.7 in rural areas and 23.5 in urban areas.

This data reveals that women's employment situation is markedly inferior to that of men, with the WPR for females being less than half of that for males in rural areas and less than one-third in urban areas.

The Time Use Survey conducted by the Ministry of Statistics and Programme Implementation (MoSPI) in 2019 shows typical patterns in the allocation of unpaid caregiving and domestic duties within households, highlighting a prominent gender disparity.

Approximately 81% of females dedicate around 5 hours daily to unpaid domestic services. This percentage is still higher at 92 for the age group 15-59 years.

Even within the 60+ age group, 78% of women contribute to unpaid domestic services.

In the 15-59 age bracket, only 29% of males participate in unpaid domestic services. The proportion of women providing unpaid caregiving services is twice that of men, with rates at 33% and 16%, respectively.

It is but obvious that a significant number of working-age women spend over six hours daily on unpaid services, while women not in the labor force invest the most time in unpaid domestic services.

Women's representation in the Central Council of Ministers has been wavering around 12, reaching its peak in 2015 (17.8%).

In comparison to the percentage of men elected to the Lok Sabha (out of total men candidates), the percentage of women elected (out of total women candidates) has always been higher.

If we consider state-wise women's participation in the 17th Lok Sabha election, among states with more than ten seats, the percentage of women MPs out of total seats was the highest in Odisha (at 33 percent) and lowest in Kerala (at 5 percent).

By proposing to reserve 33 percent of seats in the Lok Sabha and State Legislative Assemblies & the Legislative Assembly of the National Capital Territory of Delhi for women, the Women's Reservation Bill aims to address the longstanding gender disparity in political representation and decision-making bodies.

The reservation of one-third of seats for women in Panchayati Raj Institutions at the village level and one-third of the offices of the chairperson at all levels of these institutions is remarkable as well.

In the year 2023, in the Hon'ble Supreme Court of India, out of 33 judges sitting in the office, only 3 were women. In high courts also, only 14% of the judges were women. This inadequate representation of women in the judicial system warrants introspection.

Around 20% of micro, small, and medium enterprises [MSMEs] registered on the Udyam Registration Portal of the Ministry of MSME since its inception on 1st July 2020 are led by women.

To promote the sustainable development of women entrepreneurs and the linked empowerment of women, initiatives, schemes, enabling networks and communities, and activating partnerships among diverse stakeholders have been encouraged and established.

The Department for Promotion of Industry and Internal Trade (DPIIT) has recognized 117,254 start-ups from January 2016 to December 2023.

Among these, 55,816 start-ups are led by women, constituting 47.6% of the total recognized start-ups. This significant proportion of women entrepreneurs is a matter of great pride.

The number of women who are engaged in senior managerial positions in companies has also increased over the years, although it remains far less than the number of men in such positions.

In 2023-24 (up to January 2024), as many as 7.62 lakh women were on the boards of directors of companies compared to 19.75 lakh men in such posts. Similarly, 34,879 women were in senior management positions last fiscal year compared to 186,000 men.

Another 7.38 lakh women were engaged in other managerial positions last fiscal year as against 18.6 lakh men in such positions.

All the above statistical data has been taken from the document of Women & Men in India, 2023, National Statistical Office, Ministry of Statistics and Programme Implementation, Government of India, New Delhi (as mentioned above).

So, of course, India has progressed and continues to progress, and our women are being empowered in many ways while dealing with the prejudices, minor or major, being thrown at them.

Epilogue

"Don't allow men who hate women to define feminism as women who hate men."

-John Marcotte (Founder, Heroic Girls Foundation)

Dear reader, congratulations on reaching the end of my book. It's time to sit with your feelings now.

Did you at any point in time strongly identify with or relate to anything mentioned and explained in the chapters?

Also, could you see any connection between any patriarchal childhood lesson and an adulthood habit?

Did you, as a man, realize how women across generations have had to fight extra hard for basic rights and privileges?

Did you, as a woman, feel grateful to all those women because of whom we enjoy so many rights today? Did you remember a particular dream you gave up on because the people around you told you that you, being a girl, were not entitled to have that dream?

As a man, did you remember shaming a smarter woman who had achieved more than you simply because that hurt your male ego? Or did you remember how even today you struggle to cry and share when stressed and end up choosing isolation and silence?

Did you recall how you joined in and made fun of a transgender colleague just to fit in, without once thinking about what their struggles could have been?

Did you remember how your prejudiced homophobia made you distance yourself from a friend once you found out they were gay? Did they deserve that, or did they deserve freedom and friendship like every other straight person?

These and many more could be the questions and the thoughts that came to your mind.

Look around yourself and see how many people are carrying with them internalized fragments of patriarchy.

Unlearn and discard your own redundant beliefs, educate where necessary and feasible, and move towards a better future. This was the purpose of my book: to make you introspect and take action.

Remember what Alvin Eugene Toffler once said: "The illiterate of the 21st century will not be those who cannot read and write, but those who cannot learn, unlearn, and relearn."